D1301161

SURVIVAL SKILLS:

How to Handle Life's Catastrophes

SURVIVAL SKILLS:

How to Handle Life's Catastrophes

Rae Simons

Mason Crest Publishers

SURVIVAL SKILLS:
How to Handle Life's Catastrophes

MASON CREST PUBLISHERS INC.
370 Reed Road
Broomall, Pennsylvania 19008
(866)MCP-BOOK (toll free)
www.masoncrest.com

Because the stories in this series are told by real people, in some cases names
have been changed to protect the privacy of the individuals.

Portions of this book originally appeared in *The Gift of Hope: In the Wake of
the 2004 Tsunami and the 2005 Hurricanes* by Ellyn Sanna, 2006, and in *You and
the Environment* by Rae Simons, 2008. Used with permission of Village Earth
Books and AlphaHouse Publishing.

First Printing
9 8 7 6 5 4 3 2 1

ISBN 978-1-4222-0449-8 (series)
ISBN 978-1-4222-1462-6 (series) (pbk.)

Library of Congress Cataloging-in-Publication Data

Simons, Rae, 1957–
  Survival skills : how to handle life's catastrophes / by Rae
Simons.
      p. cm. — (Survivors)
  Includes bibliographical references and index.
  ISBN 978-1-4222-0456-6 (hardback : alk. paper) — ISBN
978-1-4222-1469-5 (pbk. : alk. paper)
  1. Life skills. 2. Survival skills. 3. Conduct of life. I. Title.
  HQ2037.S56 2009
  155.9'042—dc22
                                        2008050320

Design by MK Bassett-Harvey.
Produced by Harding House Publishing Service, Inc.
www.hardinghousepages.com
Cover design by Andrew Mezvinsky.
Printed in The Hashimite Kingdom of Jordan.

CONTENTS

Introduction

Each of us is confronted with challenges and hardships in our daily lives. Some of us, however, have faced extraordinary challenges and severe adversity. Those who have lived—and often thrived—through affliction, illness, pain, tragedy, cruelty, fear, and even near-death experiences are known as survivors. We have much to learn from survivors and much to admire.

Survivors fascinate us. Notice how many books, movies, and television shows focus on individuals facing—and overcoming—extreme situations. *Robinson Crusoe* is probably the earliest example of this, followed by books like the *Swiss Family Robinson*. Even the old comedy *Gilligan's Island* appealed to this fascination, and today we have everything from the Tom Hanks' movie *Castaway* to the hit reality show *Survivor* and the popular TV show *Lost*.

What is it about survivors that appeals so much to us? Perhaps it's the message of hope they give us. These people have endured extreme challenges—and they've overcome them. They're ordinary people who faced extraordinary situations. And if they can do it, just maybe we can too.

This message is an appropriate one for young adults. After all, adolescence is a time of daily challenges. Change is everywhere in their lives, demanding that they adapt and cope with a constantly shifting reality. Their bodies change in response to increasing levels of sex hormones; their thinking processes change as their brains develop, allowing them to think in more abstract ways; their social lives change as new people and peers become more important. Suddenly, they experience the burning need to form their own identities. At the same time, their emotions are labile and unpredictable. The people they were as children may seem to have disappeared beneath the onslaught of new emotions, thoughts, and sensations. Young adults have to deal with every single one of these changes, all at the same time. Like many of the survivors whose stories are told in this series, adolescents' reality is often a frightening, confusing, and unfamiliar place.

Young adults are in crises that are no less real simply because these are crises we all live through (and most of us survive!) Like all survivors, young adults emerge from their crises transformed; they are not the people they were before. Many of them bear scars they will carry with them for life—and yet these scars can be integrated into their new identities. Scars may even become sources of strength.

In this book series, young adults will have opportunities to learn from individuals faced with tremendous struggles. Each individual has her own story, her own set of circumstances and challenges, and her own way of coping and surviving. Whether facing cancer or abuse, terrorism or natural disaster, genocide or school violence, all the survivors who tell their stories in this series have found the ability and will to carry on despite the trauma. They cope, persevere, persist, and live on as a person changed forever by the ordeal and suffering they endured. They offer hope and wisdom to young adults: if these people can do it, so can they!

These books offer a broad perspective on life and its challenges. They will allow young readers to become more self-aware of the demanding and difficult situations in their own lives—while at the same time becoming more compassionate toward those who have gone through the unthinkable traumas that occur in our world.

— Andrew M. Kleiman, M.D.

Chapter One

WHAT DOES IT TAKE TO BE A SURVIVOR?

When you hear the word "survivor," what comes to mind? A woman with a pink ribbon pinned to her shirt, indicating that she's lived through breast cancer? A hit reality show, where contestants are filmed facing amazing challenges in some remote location? A tough, macho man on another TV show who battles the wilderness, using a variety of **ingenuous** resources to survive, and coming up the victor again and again? A trauma-stricken child staring into the camera after a natural disaster has torn apart her home?

In fact, all these people have something in common: they've managed to rise above a difficult set of circumstances. According to the dictionary, a survivor is "a person who has survived an ordeal or great misfortune; a

ingenuous:
cleverly inventive and resourceful.

resilient:
capable of
rebounding
from illness or
adversity.

**prefrontal
cortex:**
a part of
the brain
located at
the front; it is
involved with
intelligence
and
personality
and with
making
decisions and
weighing
good and bad
choices.

person regarded as **resilient** or courageous enough to be able to overcome hardship and misfortune." When you think about this definition, you realize something: we are all survivors of one sort or another. All of us face daily ordeals, all of us need to rise above the various challenges life gives us. Sometimes our lives are easier than others, but sooner or later, we all have various hardships and misfortunes to conquer.

AN ADOLESCENT'S LIFE

Teenagers face a particular set of challenges. Adolescence is a time of enormous change, where the very nature of reality and identity seems to shift. Some of the challenges confronting young adults include:

- body changes in response to increasing levels of sex hormones
- strong and variable emotions (also caused by hormonal changes that create overwhelming emotional reactions)
- changes in the thinking process brought on by brain development (According to recent neuroscience research, during adolescence the **prefrontal cortex** of the brain undergoes enormous upheaval and change.)
- difficulty controlling impulses (also caused by biological changes within the body)

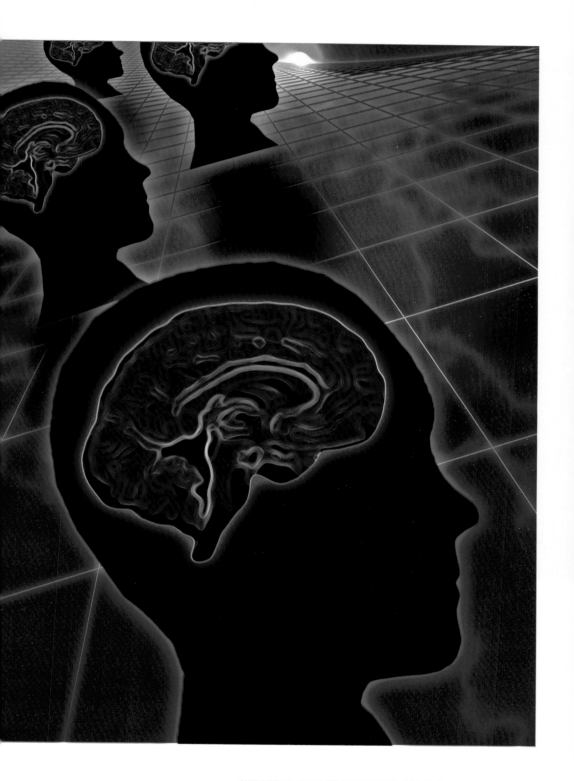

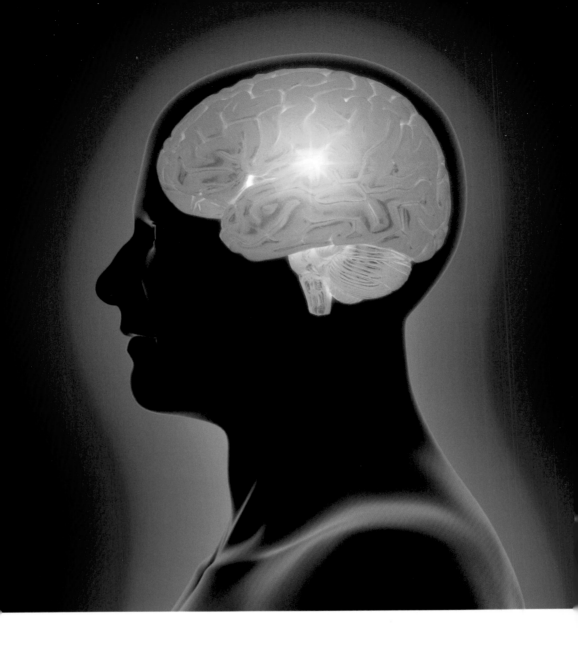

vulnerability: susceptible to being hurt.

- an increased **vulnerability** to stress and depression
- peer pressure
- the desire for new romantic relation-ships
- conflicts with parents and family

- changing expectations from the outside world

All these changes, coming all at once both from inside the individual and outside, can be overwhelming and confusing. When you're an adolescent, reality, even your very self, can seem unfamiliar and frightening. According to Victoria Tennant, an expert in teen brain development, "Teens quickly shift into survival mode when stressed. Defensive behaviors take charge and the thinking brain shuts down."

SURVIVAL MODE

Psychiatrists tell us that when we endure too much stress, we automatically switch gears into survival mode; extreme stress triggers the "fight or flight" response. Our brains' **hypothalamus** sets this response in motion, sending out a specific sequence of messages through the nervous system. These messages do a variety of things. Chemicals stream into our bloodstream, preparing our bodies to either fight—or run away. Breathing speeds up. Blood is directed away from our digestive tracts to our muscles and limbs, so that we'll have the extra energy and fuel for running or fighting. Our pupils dilate. Our senses become sharper. Our impulses come more quickly, and our perception of pain diminishes. The immune system kicks into gear, ready to fight off invaders. We're ready!

hypo-thalamus: a part of the brain that controls sleep, hunger, thirst, body temperature, and metabolism.

This response is designed to be a good thing: it's our bodies' survival plan. But the fight-or-flight system is meant to bypass our **rational** minds; after all, when you're in an emergency, you don't have time to be analyzing the meaning of the universe! This state of alert can make us perceive almost everything in our world as a possible threat to our survival—and this in turn, can make us overreact to circumstances. Our thinking may be **distorted**. Making clear choices and recognizing the consequences of those choices can become difficult. Our bodies' survival tactics were intended for coping with short-term crises, not long-term life plans.

Operating in "survival mode" can be dangerous. It can take a toll physically, emotionally, mentally, and socially, especially for teenagers, who are already facing challenges in these same four aspects of their lives.

rational: reasonable and practical.

distorted: not completely representing the truth; twisted.

SURVIVOR TEENS

Imagine a typical day in a teen's life. We'll call her Caitlin.

Caitlin wakes up at 6:30 a.m., exhausted because she was awake until after midnight the night before studying for a chemistry exam. She stumbles into the shower and gets dressed, but when she walks into the kitchen to grab some breakfast, her mother complains about the clothes Caitlin's wearing: the neckline of her tank top is too low and her jeans are hanging too low on her hips. These clothes are important to Caitlin, though—she chose them specifically for the way she wants to look today when she sees her boyfriend at lunchtime—and her mother's request that she change her clothes seems like a threat to her identity and independence. Caitlin's body picks up on the threat she's feeling, and automatically, she shifts into survival mode. She's lost all appetite for breakfast, her breathing is faster, and she reacts quickly to her mother's words with a defensive attack. Before long, she's in the midst of a full-scale fight with her mother.

An hour later, Caitlin is at school; she may or may not have won the battle over her clothes, but either way, the stress of the fight with her mother is still affecting her physically. She finds it hard to concentrate on what the teacher is saying, and her stomach hurts. Between classes, she's so relieved to be with her friends for a few minutes, that she finds herself shrieking with laughter at a joke that wasn't really all that funny. The monitor in the hallway scolds her and tells her to calm down; instantly, Caitlin is angry once more.

During lunch, she and her boyfriend have a fight, and Caitlin loses her appetite again. Her heart pounding, she goes to study hall, where she tries to study some more for her chemistry test. This is her junior year, and she needs good grades for her college applications—but the periodic table has never made much sense to her, and she's too upset and nervous to concentrate. She takes the exam

(doesn't have a clue whether she aced it or failed it), and finally heads home . . . where she discovers that her little sister has invaded her room and is reading her journal. Caitlin screams at her sister, their mother eventually intervenes, and Caitlin is furious with her mother for seeming to take her sister's side in the argument. Caitlin IMs a friend, hoping that will help her feel better, and begins to vent all the frustrations of her day. Her friend messages back that she heard through the grapevine that Caitlin's boyfriend is planning to break up with her. Caitlin bursts into tears. She calls her boyfriends on the phone. Eventually, they make up, and Caitlin feels a little better. She's still worried about their relationship, though, and she wonders how much longer it will last.

By ten o'clock, Caitlin is exhausted, but she can't sleep. Her adolescent body is wired to stay up late at night and sleep late in the morning—but unfortunately, the school day doesn't accommodate her natural sleep rhythms. She pulls out her math book and starts her homework. Eventually, around midnight, after an entire day spent in survival mode, her body collapses into unconsciousness. In the morning, she'll wake up exhausted to do it all again.

Not every day in Caitlin's life is this stressful, of course, but many of them are. Caitlin's surviving adolescence—and one day, she'll move into a new phase of her life—but the pressure is taking its toll. Physically, all this stress makes her more vulnerable to germs, so she may get sick more often. Mentally, it interferes with her ability to do her best academically. Emotionally, it's just plain painful!

Every adult in the world managed to survive adolescence, but that doesn't mean it was easy. Many adults still carry the battle scars they earned when they were teenagers. For good or bad, they'll carry them forever.

WHAT CAN SURVIVORS TEACH US?

Recently, a couple of authors have taken a closer look at what we can learn from people who have survived unusual crises such as being lost in the wilderness, natural disasters, terrorism, or cancer. They found that all these people had some things in common. Those who survived (in the sense that they truly overcame the challenges they faced) learned a set of special skills. These skills can be helpful in teenagers who are doing their best to simply survive daily life.

Laurence Gonzales, author of *Deep Survival: Who Lives, Who Dies, and Why*, believes that these skills allow the individual to not only endure hardship but to transform it into something that gives both strength and inspiration. The person is actually better because of what he has faced. Gonzales writes:

> Decades and sometimes centuries apart, separated by culture, geography, race, language, and tradition, the most successful survivors—those who practice what I call "deep survival"—go through the same patterns of thought and behavior, the same transformation and spiritual discovery, in the course of keeping themselves alive. Not only that but it doesn't seem to matter whether they are surviving being lost in the wilderness or battling cancer, whether they're

struggling through divorce or facing a business catastrophe—the strategies remain the same.

In his book, Gonzales breaks down these strategies into a twelve-point outline.

1. Perceive and Believe

"Don't fall into the deadly trap of denial," Gonzales writes. "Admit it: You're really in trouble and you're going to have to get yourself out." This means there's no good in pretending to yourself that everything is hunky-dory in your life when instead, it's really awful! But that doesn't mean you should lie down and give up either. Gonzales goes on to say:

> Survivors see opportunity, even good, in their situation, however grim. After the ordeal is over, people may be surprised to hear them say it was the best thing that ever happened to them. Viktor Frankl, who spent three years in Auschwitz and other Nazi concentration camps, describes comforting a woman who was dying. She told him, "I am grateful that fate has hit me so hard. In my former life I was spoiled and did not take spiritual accomplishments seriously."

In other words? Face reality!

2. Stay Calm, but Use Your Anger

Our bodies' normal fight-or-flight reaction can work for us or against us. Survivors learn to use their emotions to give them strength rather than allowing themselves to be overwhelmed by them. They don't whine and complain; they don't get hysterical. Instead, their emotions become the fuel to carry them forward when they're tired or discouraged. In other words, they find positive channels for their anger.

3. Think, Analyze, and Plan

"Survivors," writes Gonzales, "quickly organize, set up routines, and institute discipline." This may be difficult at a time when your body is insisting that it wants to be in control of your mind—but as Gonzales points out, a set of disciplined routines will allow you to create "a split between reason and emotion in which reason gives direction and emotion provides the power source." For someone like Caitlin, this might mean a daily exercise plan that will help her to sleep better, or setting up regular study hours earlier in the afternoon, so she can relax late at night. Each person's routines will be different, but what stays the same is the need to set aside some time to analyze the situation. (Ask yourself, "What's *really* going on here? Why am I so upset? What could I do to make this easier for myself?") Make a plan!

4. Take Correct, Decisive Action

When we're stressed, we sometimes have the tendency to feel paralyzed. We let events simply carry us along, as though life were an enormous floodwater and we were tiny twigs caught in the stream. We feel helpless. We often believe we have no choices—but we really do.

Gonzales writes:

> Survivors break down large jobs into small, manageable tasks. They set attainable goals and develop short-term plans to reach them. They are meticulous about doing those tasks well. . . . They handle what is within their power to deal with from moment to moment, hour to hour, day to day.

In other words, don't think of yourself as a victim! Take back your power.

5. Celebrate Your Success

Don't be afraid to pat yourself on the back, even for the smallest successes. When you bite your tongue and hold back an angry retort to your dad, when you pass a difficult exam, when you weather a disappointment with a friend, pay attention and allow yourself to be proud of yourself. Celebrate in some way, with a friend or by yourself. Reward yourself by allowing yourself some small treat you've been wanting.

6. Be a Rescuer

Survivors who do the best are the ones who focus not on themselves but on others. Thinking about someone else allows us to set aside our own selfish fears and worries. In other words, do whatever you can to help others!

7. Enjoy the Survival Journey

Even the most difficult situations offer moments of laughter and relief. "It may seem **counterintuitive**," writes Gonzales, "but even in the worst circumstances, survivors find something to enjoy, some way to play and laugh. . . . A playful approach to a critical situation also leads to invention, and invention may lead to a new technique, strategy, or design that could save you."

Scientists tell us that laughter stimulates an area in the brain that helps us to feel good and to be motivated, while reducing anxiety and frustration. Laughter may also trigger chemical signals that reduce fear.

In other words? Keep your sense of humor!

8. See the Beauty

When Debbie Kiley was adrift in the Atlantic Ocean after her boat sank in a hurricane, she felt she might go insane from the boredom, the fear, and the constant tension. She told herself, "Focus on the sky, on the beauty there."

Take time to look at a sunset, go for a walk in a park, or listen to your favorite music. Time spent appreciating beauty may seem

counter-intuitive: *against what common sense would lead one to believe.*

like wasted time—but scientists tell us that when we see something beautiful, our pupils actually dilate. And as our vision becomes sharper, we may also, just possibly, notice some solution to a problem that we'd previously overlooked. Noticing the world's beauty can also help us keep our own circumstances in perspective.

Gonzales points out that our awareness of this world's beauty also tends to connect us to the spiritual world. Whatever our faith, a belief in something bigger than ourselves helps us find meaning even in the midst of the most difficult days. Scientific research has found that those who pray often heal faster and cope with stress better. Connecting to something bigger—whether that's God or another human being—allows you to see past your own circumstance. "People who are deeply connected to family, friends, and the activities in their lives," says Gonzales, "people who are passionate about life, make better survivors."

9. Believe That You Will Succeed

Psychologists tell us that what we believe about ourselves often comes true. If we believe we will fail, we usually will—and if we believe we will succeed, we're far more likely to do so. Of course, our belief in ourselves needs to be rooted in reality; you can't win a marathon race, for instance, simply by believing you can do it if you never train ahead of time.

"Helping someone else is the best way to ensure your own survival. It takes you out of yourself. It helps you to rise above your fears. Now you're a rescuer, not a victim."

—Laurence Gonzales

10. Surrender

Accept the reality of your situation. Make friends with it. Stop fighting it. Resolve to learn what you can from the situation just as it is, instead of constantly fighting against it.

This may seem like the exact opposite of Gonzales' strategy #9, but actually, the two compliment each other. You can't really rise above a situation until you've accepted it.

We all have a tendency to waste our time and energy complaining and fretting, going over and over in our head all the ways our situation simply isn't fair. Life very often *isn't* fair—but pointing that out (to our friends . . . to our families . . . even to God!) won't change circumstances. There's no Judge-in-the-Sky waiting for us to bring the injustice of our circumstances to her attention so she can swoop down and set things right for us.

Once you surrender to the circumstances—whether it's the fact that your girlfriend wants to break up with you, that you didn't make the football team, or that your little brother really bugs you—then you have more energy left for finding new solutions, discovering new insights, and becoming a survivor who has grown into a better person.

11. Do Whatever Is Necessary

Survivors aren't squeamish. They eat bugs, drink their own urine, cut off body parts, take chemotherapy, and do a variety of other unpleasant things that most of us would never even consider doing. As a teenager facing the challenges of life, fortunately, you're not likely to have to do any of those things. Instead, you might have to be embarrassed . . . or give up something important to you . . . or learn to wait for something you want very much.

12. Never Give Up

"Survivors," writes Gonzales, "are not easily discouraged by setbacks."

> They accept that the environment is constantly changing and know that they must adapt. When they fall, they pick themselves up and start the entire process over again, breaking it down into manageable bits.

Author Amanda Ripley has also written a book on what it takes be a survivor. Hers is titled *The Unthinkable: Who Survives When Disaster Strikes—and Why*. Like Gonzales, Ripley believes that survivors have important skills to teach us. What's more, she indicates that these are skills we can all practice, teaching ourselves to be survivors in the truest sense of the word, even when faced with challenges that seem like way too much for us to handle. She quotes Peter Hancock who studies human performance for the U.S. military:

> "If an engineer wants to know about what he's designing, he puts it under

"Everybody has a mountain to climb. Everybody has a wilderness inside."

—Laurence Gonzales

This soldier builds a fire to help combat frostbite and hypothermia during a winter survival situation. Survivors know what has to be done and never give up, even when challenges are especially tough.

great amounts of stress. . . . It's the same with human beings." . . . Without too much trouble, we can teach our brains to work more quickly, maybe even more wisely, under great stress. We have more control over our fates than we think. But we need to stop underestimating ourselves.

Are you underestimating yourself? Start thinking of yourself as a survivor, someone who puts all these skills into practice daily. Ripley also includes this quote in her book:

"Skill is my ability to do something automatically, at the subconscious level. I don't have to think about it. It's programmed. How do I get that? I do that by repetition, by practicing the right thing."

As you read the stories and advice from survivors included in the chapters that follow, make your own survival plan. Pay attention to ways you can carry over the skills learned in these extreme situations into your own life. And then put those skills to use.

"Practice makes perfect," your grandmother probably told you. She was right.

Chapter Two

FACE REALITY

You might think that if you were living in the midst of an abusive relationship it wouldn't be all that difficult to recognize. A woman named Laura, however, has learned otherwise. And until she was willing to face reality, she couldn't begin to be a true survivor.

Laura had never thought of herself as the victim of abuse. Like many women who find themselves with an abusive partner, she just thought that her husband Gary had a particularly bad temper, the same way her dad did. And sometimes, when Gary got mad, he'd take it out on her. For a long time, it seemed pretty normal to her.

"It was normal for us for the man to abuse," Laura said. "My dad would beat us all the time." It was also normal for Laura to see the "man of the house" doing a lot of drinking. So when Gary got drunk and began to hit her, Laura thought it was just something men did, something to be expected.

Laura and Gary had been girlfriend and boyfriend in high school. They got married when they were very young, and Laura became pregnant. The "problem," said Laura, didn't start until after their first child was born. Although, come to think of it, she recalls, Gary had given her a pretty hard shove once when she was pregnant. . . .

But she hadn't thought anything of it. Even when Gary started hitting her, the abuse wasn't constant. For every six months of abuse, there would be six months of calm. She thought that was normal for a young married couple, just part of the ups and downs of marriage.

Laura can see now, however, that even before Gary's physical abuse began, from the very beginning he was psychologically abusive. Like most abusers, he found her weaknesses and poked at them. For instance, he knew she was ashamed of her upbringing, that she wondered whether she was "good enough" for Gary. Gary used this knowledge to whittle away at her self-esteem. He often told her she was from the "wrong side of the tracks" and that she should feel privileged to be with him. Because the things he said reinforced fears she already had, Laura mistook Gary's psychological abuse for the truth.

He's right, she would think. *I don't deserve him. I need to "be on my best behavior" so as not to lose him.* Her belief that Gary was better than her made her willing to put up with his anger. Deep inside, a part of her believed she deserved it.

Until years after Laura left Gary, she did not fully understand all the ways her husband had been abusive to her from day one. "When you're in the middle of your life," she said, "it's often difficult to see clearly what's going on. With time and reflection, comes clarity. There's no point beating yourself up over knowledge you didn't have until later!"

After a few years of marriage and the birth of their first child, Gary's abuse had **escalated** from psychological to **intermittent** physical to intense physical abuse. His new favorite method of abuse was to choke his wife. Like many abusers, he always did it very carefully, making sure he never left a mark.

During one particularly **traumatic** act of violence, Gary raped Laura. When Laura became pregnant as a result, Gary tried to force her to get an abortion. Laura refused—and Gary pushed her down the stairs, hoping to cause a miscarriage. Both Laura and the baby survived, but Laura was truly frightened now.

Gary had been abusing alcohol for years, but later in the marriage, he turned to cocaine, LSD, and heroin. This combination of narcotics seemed to increase Gary's

escalated: increased in amount or intensity.

intermittent: stopping and starting periodically.

traumatic: resulting in injury to the body; also, psychologically painful.

Talking to a counselor is usually very helpful for women who have been sexually abused. Counselors provide a more realistic viewpoint of the situation and can help the women cope with emotional issues.

abusive behavior. Before long, he went from beating his wife to beating his children. During one incident, Gary grabbed his son by the throat, threw him across the room, and then demanded, "Get up and fight for yourself!" Laura was horrified.

Over the years, Laura had endured so much physical and psychological pain inflicted by her husband that she'd almost come to take it for granted. Now, however, when she witnessed her husband's attack on their son, something clicked in her brain. Maybe she hadn't loved herself enough to put an end to her own abuse—but she did love her children.

For a long time, everyone who loved Laura had wanted her to leave her husband—but until now, she hadn't been ready. For many victims of abuse, a single turning point finally pushes them to say, "Enough is enough!" Laura had reached that point: seeing her husband abuse their child was the final straw. She finally faced reality. It wasn't easy. In fact, it was scary and painful. But once she had faced the facts—she was married to an abusive man—she knew she had to leave.

Laura's Additional Survival Skills for Teens

- If you're not strong enough yet to face reality for yourself, do it for someone you love. And then learn to love yourself!

- Don't feel guilty that you couldn't face reality sooner. We all do the best we can, and guilt doesn't accomplish anything. Forgive yourself and move on.

Chapter Three

FIND POSITIVE CHANNELS FOR YOUR ANGER

Klee, Jeneda, and Clayson Benally are Blackfire, a punk rock group that has toured around the world. These two brothers and a sister are also survivors of racial prejudice. Their father is Diné, and their mother is descended from a mixture of Polish Jew and Russian Gypsy; her descendents fled to America in 1912 to escape racial persecution in the "Old Country." The younger generation of Benallys has also had to come to terms with racism in their own lives.

Their first encounter with racial prejudice came when they went off the **reservation** to attend high school. "I didn't understand," Jeneda says. "I went from being a 4.0 student to getting poor grades. All the cliques were determined by race. It was heartbreaking. I

reservation: a piece of public land set aside for a special purpose, such as for use by an Indian tribe.

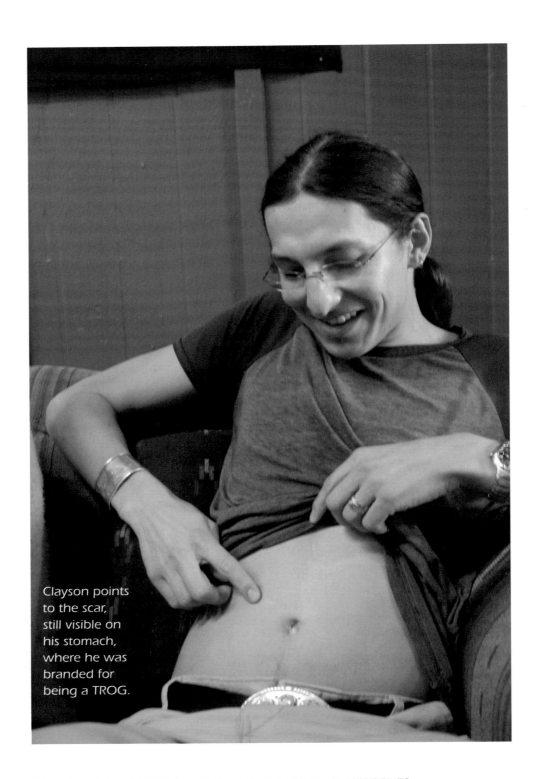

Clayson points to the scar, still visible on his stomach, where he was branded for being a TROG.

wanted to drop out of school. We'd grown up in an environment where differences were celebrated rather than discriminated." Klee agrees that once he went off the reservation to high school, he was pressured to conform, to become something he wasn't in order to fit in. "'I want to cut my hair,' I told our parents. 'Why can't I?'" Clayson, the youngest Benally sibling, was also teased at school because he wore his hair long, as is traditional for Diné males. He wanted to join the track team, but he was told he couldn't unless he cut his hair. Other students called him a TROG—a Total Reject of God. They even went so far as to hold him down and brand his stomach with a lighter.

"People don't want to believe it," Jeneda says, "but racism is real. There are stores where Native people don't go because they know if they do, they'll be ignored. When my father was younger, people would outright say to him, 'We don't serve your kind.' There used to be signs in stores that said, 'No dogs or Indians allowed.'"

preconditioned: prepared in advance.

Racism, say the Benallys, hurts the identity of both individuals and communities. "You become **preconditioned** to accept what is told you," Jeneda says. "You see yourself as weak, as a victim. You become **disempowered**. You don't see your culture reflected in the popular media, on television, in movies, in the music, and so you question your identity."

disempowered: having been deprived of power or influence.

"At first," Klee says, "you ask, 'Why is this happening to our people?' But then you move past that. You say, 'What can we do about it?'"

For the Benallys, their punk group Blackfire is a tool they use to speak out on behalf of their community. Blackfire's music brings a powerful message to people's attention.

FINDING YOUR VOICE

Klee Benally is angry. You hear his rage in his music, you see it in his face, and you understand it when you listen to his words. He has good reason to be angry—and he puts his anger to good use.

"Anger is a powerful tool," he says. "And it is part of the healing process. But anger does not equal vengeance. Anger needs to be channeled. When it becomes a negative force, something that leads to violence, it has no positive effect on anyone. When you fuel your creativity with your anger, though, you empower yourself. Positive channels for anger open eyes, minds, and heart to others' experiences. It educates people and brings awareness. Use your voice. Be creative. Find the connections between us. That's what Blackfire is doing."

As the Benallys travel around the world, performing their music in many different nations to many different groups of people, they have opportunities to share with other racial minorities. They encourage young people around the world to empower themselves with creative self-expression. "Once you put forth your intention to address something," Klee believes, "once you **articulate** the questions, you can begin to make change."

articulate: *say clearly and distinctly.*

CONNECTING TO THE COMMUNITY

Lack of self-respect hurts not only the individual but also the community—but creativity builds communities. "Creativity is a **collaborative** act," says Klee. "It allows us to come together with others."

collaborative: *achieved by working together as a joint effort.*

Klee believes that a connection to the community is vital for those who face racial prejudice. "When we are isolated," he says, "we become desperate, and desperation leads to violence, both toward others and against ourselves. Connecting our individual experiences to the community's past gives us strength. The weight of racism is too heavy. No person should have to carry this package alone." As people come together, both individuals and communities are strengthened.

"It's an easy recipe," Klee says. "Respect is the key ingredient. The first step is to articulate the justice for yourself. The second step is to communicate this to others. Don't keep it inside. Don't let it isolate you. Use your anger to build bridges, make connections, within your own community and then from your community to other communities." Communication leads to understanding, Klee explains, and understanding leads to respect. "But the circle can go the other way:

The Benallys' Additional Survival Skills for Teens

- Find your voice. Make yourself heard.

- Use your creativity to channel your anger—and to make a difference in the world.

- Connect with others. Hardship and challenges are easier to bear when they're shared.

isolation leads to ignorance, which creates fear, which contributes to racism."

Klee wants young people to know they can convert their anger into energy that can achieve something positive. "Confront discrimination where you see it. Look for ways to reconnect the positive circle—and break the negative one. . . . Look at the suffering of other people," Klee tells us. "Ask yourself, how can that be justified? How can we be **complacent**? How can we continue making choices that underpin the suffering of other people? We have the responsibility to take a stand when we see injustice happening."

complacent: contented, unconcerned.

TRANSFORMING ANGER

Before the Benallys' maternal ancestors left Russia, a man stormed into their house brandishing an ax, ready to kill them simply because they belonged to a different ethnic group. Their great-grandmother must have been terrified, but she took a stand that surprised the man. "You must be hungry," she said to him. "Won't you sit down and eat with us?"

The man's ax was bloody from the murders he'd just committed in eight other homes, but now he put it down. He shared a meal with the family, and when he left their home, he left behind the ax. "We still have that ax," Jeneda says. It's an important symbol to Klee, Jeneda, and Clayson about what is most important to their family.

"The moment we take a stand is the moment we become part of the solution," Klee says. "We become the answer, the hope. . . . Wounds do heal. We are invited to be healers—to become the tools that make a difference."

Sometimes, just one person can transform anger into a force that can change the world.

Chapter Four

MAKE A
PLAN

N oy is a woman who lives on a tiny island off the coast of Thailand. She is a member of a sea gypsy community that has endured for centuries. But on December 26, 2004, when an enormous tsunami swept across the Indian Ocean, Noy's village changed forever.

The Moken sea gypsies have lived on the Indian Ocean for as long as they remember. Once entire families spent their lives in long wooden boats, fishing with spears and nets, following the cycles of moon and **monsoon**. Their boats were their second bodies, the vessels that carried them through life, and the sea was their home, their element, as vital to their existence as the air they breathed. The Moken believed everything had a soul: the water, their boats, the trees and plants that grew on

monsoon: a seasonal wind in the Indian Ocean and southern Asia that in India and adjacent areas is characterized by heavy rainfall.

hierarchy:
a division or
classification
of society
according to
economic,
social, or
professional
standing.

the islands, the wind and sky and sun. They
had no concept of land ownership, no understanding of an economy based on money, and
no **hierarchy** in their minds built on the words
"rich" and "poor." Instead, their world was
alive and friendly. Their connection to it was
a simple fact of their daily lives.

But as the world changed, the Moken
learned that if they kept to their ancient ways,
spending only a few months on land, they soon
had no place where they could return from the
sea during the monsoons' storms. The islands
in the Indian Ocean were a growing attraction
for tourists from around the world, and the
Moken could no longer assume their huts on
stilts would be waiting for them when they
came in from the sea. **Squatters' rights** were
their only security, and many of the Moken
moved into their land houses and settled
down, fishing the waters near the islands by
day but sleeping on dry land.

**Squatters'
rights:**
the legal
allowance to
use a property
because
you are
continuously
living in it.

Gradually, the Moken adapted to contact
with the rest of the world. They spoke their
own language, but they learned other lan-
guages as well. They still ate mostly fish and
the wild fruit and vegetables that grew on the
islands, but now they also traded their fish
for rice. Money had little place in their lives,
Noy said. Coins and bills were for buying
something pretty for a baby, a gold bracelet
or a silver bangle. The sea and the land provided everything they truly needed.

They made their boats and knit their nets
and fashioned traps for shrimp and crabs just

Noy's husband Nong, one of the Moken islanders, repairs his nets.

as their ancestors had. But gasoline motors made their boats go faster, so that the men could follow the fish and get back home to their wives and children. And engines and gasoline cost money, which meant they now needed to catch enough fish and shrimp to sell to the tourist resorts—and still have enough left over to feed their families.

But still the men went out to sea and fished, while the women stayed behind to share the responsibilities of food preparation and child care. The young children played in the space between the huts, and the older ones went with their fathers to help with the

Noy, a member of the Moken sea gypsy community, demonstrates a crab trap made by her family.

catch. Houses were places for sleeping; the outdoors was where the community worked and talked and played. Food was everywhere, both on land and in the sea; garbage was nonexistent, because shells and husks degrade naturally; and the patterns of sun and moon, earth and sea were endlessly fascinating, more entertaining than any television drama. Their life was slow and simple and satisfying.

And then came the morning of December 26, 2004. With no money, no savings, no permanent possessions, the Moken were vulnerable. After the disaster, relief aid swept in from around the world, and the Moken were moved to temporary housing on the mainland. In effect, though, their lives were struck by two tsunamis: the first was a natural disaster caused by an earthquake deep below the ocean, but the second was a tidal wave of modern culture. Suddenly, they were exposed to a totally different way of living, a way that was built on cash and coins, on paper and plastic, on jobs and debt, bank accounts and possessions. "We learned we were poor," said Noy.

The Moken people on Noy's island lost their boats in the tsunami. Forced now to rent boats, their catch each month brought in barely enough money to cover their rent payments, let alone to provide for their families. And at the same time, they were threatened with the loss of something even more valuable: their culture.

mangroves: coastal tropical trees or shrubs of the genus Rhizophora that send out dense masses of roots, which serve as unique and vital ecosystems; they are important in preventing coastal erosion and actually aid in rebuilding coastal land.

incongruous: inconsistent; mismatched.

If you were to visit Noy's island, you would travel there in a small fishing boat that would carry you across the sea and into the island's muddy channels. You would see fishing nets, small houses built on stilts, **mangroves** hung with spider webs. When you climbed on land, the villagers would watch you from the shadows beneath the trees. You might be impressed by how clean and American the children looked in their bright, new T-shirts emblazed with Mickey Mouse and Cookie Monster. Their clothing had all been given to them after the tsunami, you'd learn, donations from people from around the world. You'd see piles of cardboard juice boxes outside the thatched houses, and heaps of plastic milk bottles scattered across the sand. (There is no trash collection on Noy's island, and no boat to carry it away if there were.) Small solar panels next to each home would seem **incongruous**, high-tech reminders of another world.

"The government installed them," Noy explained, "so that we can have electricity. So that we can have televisions—and if there is another tsunami, we will be able to hear the warning." She shrugged. "Now our children want to watch television instead of go to school. But if they do not go to school, the government will close the school. And if we have no school here, the government will send our children to a boarding school on the mainland." She shook her head. "We will not be separated from our children. But we cannot lose our life here on the island either. It is hard for people to see what needs to be done.

"Before the tsunami, we were like children," she continued. "We didn't think about

A solar panel installed by the Thai government provides electricity to the thatched house that stands nearby.

how we lived. We didn't pay attention to the choices we made. We just did what made us happy. Now we need a plan."

She pointed with pride to the wild orchids and other flowers she plants around her home, and she laughed as she described the culture shock she faced when the government moved the villagers to temporary housing on the mainland. (On one occasion, she and several other villagers were "trapped" in an elevator, not knowing they should push a button; another time, she nearly lost her sarong in a revolving door.)

"We couldn't stay on the mainland," she continued. "We don't belong there. We would stop being ourselves if we stayed. But since the tsunami, everything is different. We have a chance to build ourselves something better—or we could lose everything. We have to think carefully. We have to pay attention to what is most important to us. The choices we make are important."

Noy spoke at length of the way life had been before the tsunami, the closeness they had shared, the joy the sea had given them. When the tsunami came, many of the Moken villages were completely destroyed, and their residents now live in temporary government

Noy's Additional Survivor Skills for Teens

- Pay attention to what is most important to you.

- Make careful choices based on that.

housing on the mainland. Noy's village, however, was far enough inland that the houses still stand. "The government wanted us to stay on the mainland," she said. "And some of us were afraid to come back. But us," she waved her hand around the ragged circle of houses, "we knew we had to come back, even if the government didn't want us to. If there is another tsunami, my husband and I will not leave again. If we give up our homes, we will give up our lives."

Noy knows what she wants in life, and she knows what she needs to do to achieve it. She's a survivor with a plan.

DER EWIGE JUDE

EIN DOKUMENTARFILM ÜBER DAS WELTJUDENTUM

Chapter Five

DON'T THINK OF YOURSELF AS A VICTIM

Abram Korn grew up in Lipno, Poland, where his family owned a small lumberyard just outside of town. They were active in the Jewish community there, and life was peaceful. Then, when he was sixteen years old, the Nazis invaded Poland and everything changed.

At first, his father tried to organize the community to resist the Nazi invaders. Soon, though, it was clear that the Nazis were more interested in hurting the Jews than the rest of the Polish community. The non-Jewish Poles began turning against their Jewish friends and neighbors. When the Nazis took the lumberyard, and the Korn family heard that all Jews in Lipno were soon to be deported to the Warsaw ghetto, they knew they needed to get out.

In a horse-drawn wagon, Abe's parents and his two sisters, Gitel and Mirjam, left Lipno and traveled to the town of Ostrowy, not far away. Abe stayed in Lipno for a little while longer, putting their furniture and belongings in storage. The family still believed they would be able to come home soon, when the craziness with the Nazis had blown over.

In Ostrowy, the Abe and his family stayed with relatives, but nowhere was safe from the Nazis anymore. They had been in Ostrowy only a short time when all the Jews in the town were rounded up and deported to the Kutno ghetto.

The ghetto in Kutno was a terrible place, with conditions that quickly went from bad to

The main square of the Kutno ghetto was muddy and filthy.

worse. Several thousand Jews lived together in a dilapidated former sugar factory. One open-pit toilet served them all, and one hand pump for water. The toilet was never cleaned out so that it eventually overflowed, adding to the general misery. The ghetto was walled up, sealing the Jews in so that no one could get in or out, no one could escape from their dismal prison.

It was winter by the time Abe and his family arrived in Kutno. The factory had no real heat and no good place to sleep. People survived as well as they could, but the death rates were extremely high. The food rations provided by the Nazis were nowhere near enough to prevent eventual starvation. Diseases swept through the dirty, overcrowded ghetto, killing hundreds.

After a year in Kutno, Abe knew he needed to get out if he was going to survive and if he was going to help his family to survive. His mother did not want him to go at first, but his father convinced her it was the right thing for them all. His goodbyes were emotional, not knowing whether he would ever see his family again:

> My heart broke as the moment of departure and separation from my family neared. I ran to meet the outstretched arms of my mother. Her frail, weakened form convulsed with sobs as she embraced me and kissed me goodbye. She held on to me with a grip

that expressed volumes. It said, "Go." It said, "Stay." It said, "How sad." It said, "How much I love you, now and forever." It said, "God, please watch over my son." It said the unspeakable. It spoke of a mother's love for her only son. My sisters cried and held on to me as if to hold on to the memory of this moment—and to life. . . . I had to summon all my strength to make my feet take me away. I was never to see my family again.

Together with his friend Garfingal, Abe bribed a guard to let them out of Kutno, and they walked to the next town, Krosniewice. Krosniewice also had a ghetto, but unlike Kutno it was not enclosed by walls. Since the conditions were a little better, Abe was able to find work through the Nazis—who sometimes hired Jews to do certain heavy labor jobs—and was able to send a little food back to his family in Kutno.

Early the next year, 1941, the men of the Krosniewice ghetto were deported to Camp Hardt, a labor camp. Like the ghettos, the conditions were bad and food was extremely scarce, but here people were expected to work all day to earn their meager ration. Abe watched as men around him collapsed and died from exhaustion and hunger. Watching, he determined to do whatever it took to survive. He saw that the lives of the Jewish prisoners meant nothing to the Nazi guards; if

These children stand homeless in the Warsaw ghetto during the winter of 1940.

a prisoner could not work or caused trouble for them in any way, the guards simply shot him without a second thought. Abe realized that he needed to stay useful to the Nazis if he was going to survive.

After a year at Camp Hardt, Abe was sent to the concentration camp at Gross-

Rosen, where conditions were much, much worse:

> We heard a whistle and shouts of *schnell* (hurry), as the Nazis ordered us to line up. My eyes beheld an unbelievable sight. Men were running around barefoot in the snow, as though they were going out of their minds. With emaciated bodies, they did not look like human beings anymore. My thoughts went far afield. What has happened to these people? What will happen to me? Why did they send me here, and how did I get into this position?

Abe knew he could not live long at Gross-Rosen. To survive, he would have to do whatever he could to get out of there. Before he had left his family in the Kutno ghetto, his father had insisted he bring a new pair of shoes, and now he was able to use these shoes to bribe a guard to let him on the next transport out of the camp.

Surprisingly, he and the other men leaving the camp were put on the train's passenger cars. The other times he had been transported between camps, the prisoners had been packed into cattle cars, but now they

Jews from the Lublin ghetto are hurried onto trains where they will be taken to the Sobibor death camp.

were able to sit on seats and look out the windows, like the humans that they were.

This better treatment continued when Abe and the other prisoners arrived at Camp Dretz, near Berlin. Camp Dretz was a work camp, but not a concentration camp. Abe was given good food, and he grew stronger and healthier here. When he worked, he mingled with German civilians, who treated him as an equal. This experience helped Abe believe that not all Germans were cruel and anti-Semitic like the Nazis.

In April of 1943, Abe was **deported** again, along with all the other prisoners from Camp Dretz. For two days, they stood in a cattle car, packed so tightly they couldn't sit down and could barely breathe. There was no food, no water, no place to go to the bathroom.

deported: transported out of an area, often through force.

The train stopped and the prisoners breathed a sigh of relief. Now, they thought, we will finally be able to at least breathe fresh air. But there was no relief, and the air was hardly fresh. They had arrived at Birkenau, part of the **infamous** death camp of Auschwitz. Not far from the train station, the smoke from the **crematoriums** blackened the sky, filling the air with the stench of burning bodies.

infamous: having a very bad reputation.

crematoriums: furnaces used to burn dead bodies.

Most died quickly at Auschwitz. If they survived the selections, where hundreds of thousands were sent directly to the gas chambers, they then had to face beatings, starvation, and exhaustion. Abe, arriving from Camp Dretz, was in better condition than many of the prisoners. He soon learned there was a system in Auschwitz to get the food and supplies that were needed. He stole from the Nazis and then, when he was sent on work details outside the camp, he traded the stolen goods with people living nearby.

With his determination to survive, and to make a life for himself however horrible the circumstances, Abe lived for nearly two years in Auschwitz. Then, in January 1945, the Nazis **evacuated** the camp. The war was not going well for the Nazis, and the Allied forces were pushing closer every day.

evacuated: removed all people from a place; emptied out.

Abe and thousands of other prisoners were forced onto a death march, walking for over a month through the snow. All around him, people died. Anyone who stopped to rest was shot. Freezing, starving, and exhausted, people collapsed, not caring whether they lived or died. Abe kept marching, determined not to give up. His feet had swollen from frostbite and gangrene, and he could no longer force his shoes on. When they finally reached Buchenwald Concentration Camp, in the center of Germany, only two hundred were left of the two thousand who had started the death march in Abe's group.

As the Allies closed in, the Nazis evacuated the camps, marching everyone who might still be useful to them for days at a time to camps further inside Germany.

Abe was very sick. Because it was clear he could not work, he was put with other prisoners the Nazis did not think were worth treating, since it was clear they would die anyway. Abe's survival, once again, depended on being able to convince the Nazis he could be useful to them. He was able to argue that he would soon be able to work again and got himself transferred to the infirmary, where he got some medical treatment, although not enough. By this point in the war, the Nazis resources were very sparse, and prisoners were not a high priority.

On April 11, 1945, Abe was lying in his bunk, too sick to get up, when he suddenly heard singing. He thought he must be imagining things, but suddenly the door were flung open:

> I finally believed my ears because my eyes saw a sight I shall never forget. I beheld a miracle. Some of the same German SS officers from whom we had taken orders but moments before, now

These men in Buchenwald stand in one of the endless roll calls.

marched into our barracks with their hands and bodies bound in rope. . . .

Behind the singing prisoners came the American soldiers. It was unbelievable, but it was true. We had done everything in our power to stay alive long enough to see Liberation, despite so many designed traps to annihilate us. We were finally seeing the miracle happen.

Abe had survived years of persecution, imprisonment, starvation, and exhaustion. He had been determined not to give up, not to let the Nazis break his spirit. At the same time, he refused to let his pride stand in the way of his survival. He saw that if he was useful to the Nazis, he would live longer and he did what he could to convince them that he was useful, even when he was so sick he could only huddle on a bunk. He refused to sit back **passively** and let his future be decided without his input. He escaped from Kutno ghetto and smuggled food back in. Later, the entire population of Kutno, including Abe's family, was deported to the

---

Abe's Additional Survival Skills for Teens

- Be determined.

- Don't be passive.

- Don't let your pride stand in your way.

- Don't believe everyone is bad; look for those who are kind and good.

---

passively: without action or resistance.

Chelmo extermination camp and killed. Abe was young and, for much of the war, strong and healthy. He was able to work hard, steal, trade, smuggle, and bribe guards.

Throughout his ordeal, Abe refused to think of himself as a victim. He refused to believe all Germans were evil, and, in fact, married a German girl after the war. His son later wrote that his father "never lost his dignity or his love for his fellow man, even though he lived through some of the most horrible life experiences imaginable." His story is the story of life.

Chapter Six

CELEBRATE
YOUR
SUCCESS

Brittany is a cancer survivor. Here is her story:

I grew up in a neighborhood full of tough, sports-playing boys and the only way I was going to fit in with them was if I could learn to keep up. So I did. I was out there every day playing kickball, football, baseball, anything. I absolutely love playing sports and I am the type of girl, who would rather play football in the mud than go shopping at the mall.

Before June of 2005 sports were what my life was about. I played soccer for school, a travel team, and was on both the indoor and outdoor track teams for my high school. I even made varsity track as an eighth-grader. I have always been the girl that none of the boys wanted to race in gym class for the simple reason that no boy wanted to "lose to a girl."

Then in June 2005 everything changed. I first noticed there was something wrong after running in a track meet. My knee didn't feel right. I went to see the athletic trainer and began physical therapy because we thought it was just a pulled muscle. It never crossed my mind that it could be cancer, and when the doctors told me that I had osteosarcoma, a bone cancer, my world fell apart.

The tumor was just above my right knee. Everything was a blur, and I never fully accepted or understood how much it was going to change my life. I was told that I would need **chemotherapy**, surgery, then even more chemotherapy, and that I would have to start right away. I wasn't even allowed to finish the school year.

All my treatments had to be done as an **inpatient**, so I spent most of my time at Golisano Children's Hospital at Strong Hospital in Rochester, New York, almost every weekend, usually going in on Fridays and leaving on Monday, only to come back again the following Friday.

I also had some unexpected hospital stays because of fevers and low blood counts. On December 23, 2004, my six-

chemo-therapy: treatment with strong drugs that destroy quickly multiplying cancer cells, or make them less active.

inpatient: treatment done at a hospital requiring at least one overnight stay.

teenth birthday, I woke up with a fever and ended up in the hospital for six days getting blood and **platelet transfusions**. It was not my first choice of places to be on my "sweet 16," let alone Christmas, but everyone at the hospital, as well as my family and best friend Charla, did a great job making sure it was still special for me.

platelet:
tiny cells floating in the blood shaped like disks or plates that are produced in the bone marrow; their main function is to prevent bleeding by assisting with blood clotting.

transfusions:
transfers of blood or blood products from one person to another.

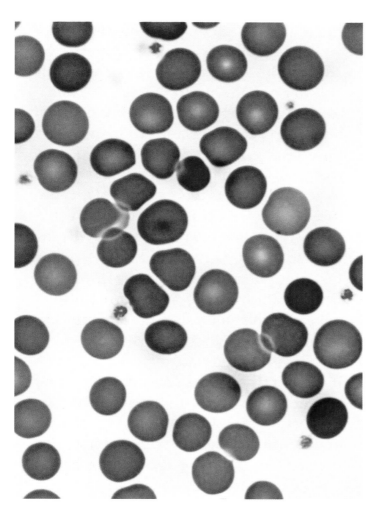

Platelets are the tiny cells in blood that cause your blood to clot if you are cut. Cancer treatment can interfere with normal platelet levels.

oncology:
the study
of the
development,
diagnosis,
and treatment
of cancerous
tumors.

**social
worker:**
someone
who works
to provide
social services
to those
dealing with
serious illness
or economic
disadvantages.

One of the really good things about Golisano Children's Hospital is the people who work there: the nurses, doctors, and the oncology social worker Eric Iglewski. They became like family, and they were all absolutely wonderful, knowing exactly what to do or say to make my day a little brighter. Some of them were quite entertaining too. The only hard part about ending chemotherapy was saying good-bye to all of them.

I had limb-salvage surgery on August 30, 2005, the extent of which is still overwhelming to me. It's the hardest thing I had to deal with. I had a total knee replacement, and rods replaced part of my upper and lower leg. The recovery was hard; there are no words to fully describe the extreme pain. But the physical pain is easy compared to the emotional pain that comes with the new rules I now have to live by for the rest of my life: no running or impact on my leg! For me this means my life will never be the same. No more track and no more soccer.

I was blindsided by this and took it harder than finding out that I had cancer. Right up to the moment before surgery, I prayed it was all a big mistake and I wouldn't need the surgery. I even threatened my parents with running

away just to keep my knee so I could play soccer.

I have to fight back the tears every time I visit the track or soccer field. Sometimes it's really hard and I have to turn back before I even get there. My coaches and teammates have all been very supportive. At first I tried to remain an active member of all my teams, but it

Chemotherapy is often administered intravenously. Drugs that kill cancer go directly into a vein.

biopsy: surgical procedures performed to diagnose and identify many different types of cancer.

remission: when cancer responds to treatment or is brought under control; in complete remission all signs and symptoms of the disease disappear.

was too hard to deal with, so I found a new way to remain active in sports; I am helping to coach a girl's travel soccer team for the local Soccer Association and I love every minute of it. Even though I cannot play, my love for soccer and track will never go away.

The good news is that after surgery the **biopsy** showed that the chemotherapy worked. One hundred percent of the cancer cells had been killed! The day I heard that, I knew everything would be okay. I am now in **remission** and get scans every three months to make sure the cancer has not returned. We celebrated my one-year-off-treatment anniversary in February with a party. It's almost like having two birthdays to celebrate. Every day, I thank God that I have my life back and get to do normal teenage stuff.

As hard as this has all been, many good things have come out of it. I have met so many amazing people and learned so much about myself and how precious life is. I will never complain about a bad hair day again! I also connected with

Brittany's Additional Survival Skills for Teens

- Don't be afraid to grieve for your losses.

- Find the good that comes with the bad.

- Make the best of every situation.

- Live life to the fullest.

an organization called Teens Living with Cancer, which allows me to meet other teens with cancer. That has been very inspiring to me. I am lucky because my friends stayed by my side and supported me during my treatment, but no one can understand what I have been through like another teen with cancer can.

I have no idea what the future holds, but there is one thing I know for sure: I will make the best of every situation and live life to the fullest. I kicked cancer. I can do anything!

Chapter Seven

HELP OTHERS

T he morning of Sunday, December 26, 2004, dawned clear and serene. Prasit Sathaphonchaturawit, the director of the Bangsak School in Thailand's Phang-Nga Province, woke early, just as he always did, and stepped outside to breathe the air. With a sense of contentment, he ate his breakfast and then drove to the school. The sun glimmered through the trees off the ocean as he got out of his car.

Prasit smiled as he walked down the school's empty corridor and went into his office. His life pleased him: there was his desk, piled with work; his office walls were hung with pictures of students' activities to encourage him with the reason for his work; and contest certificates and sport trophies reminded him of his school's successes. Prasit sat down at his desk;

by noon, he hoped to have made his way through at least half the stack of papers.

But his concentration was disturbed by shouts outside the school building. The voices grew louder, and Prasit got up to look out the window. Streaming past the school was a jittery mass of human beings, climbing as fast as they could toward higher land. With a sense of unreality, he heard them screaming for their children, crying for help, sobbing.

And then Prasit turned his gaze in the opposite direction, toward the trees through which he normally glimpsed the shining ocean. Instead, he saw a wall of water taller than the trees. Without further thought, he rushed to his car.

Too late. The water had already heaved his car into the air. A breath later, it snatched Prasit and threw him upward, like an enormous hand tossing a ball. As the school disappeared beneath the immense wave, a tall, deeply rooted tree caught Prasit in its branches. A few minutes later, his desk chair landed on the branch beside him.

Prasit found himself surveying a nightmare. Below him was a wide sea strewn with mangled cars pushed up against the ruined walls of his school. The Thai flag still fluttered from a flagpole, but everything else was gone.

Two more enormous waves surged around Prasit's tree—and then, just as suddenly as it had come, the water sucked backward. "I felt as though I had popped through a hole from one reality into another," Prasit said. When he climbed down his tree, the new reality he found was the most awful thing he had ever seen. Everywhere he looked, dead bodies were scattered in the mud and debris. His entire world had been washed away. He stood silent, shaking, staring, and thanked God that no students or teachers had been in the school.

But thirty-eight members of Prasit's family died that day.

The next day, Prasit was back at the school site. People were searching through the

This child lost his father in the tsunami—but Prasit's rebuilt school offers him both a home and a place to learn.

debris, seeking their loved ones, sunbathers and beachcombers who had been caught by the tsunami and washed up on the school grounds. He knew that many of his students had lost their lives; some had lost their parents; still others had lost their homes, their security, their families' livelihoods.

And yet life must go on, Prasit told himself. He could not stand grieving over the tragedy; if he did, he would give the disaster more destructive power than it **merited**. Instead, he said, "I renewed my commitment to the school."

With the help of the school staff, Prasit gathered the remaining students and set up classrooms in the garage and backyard of a teacher's house. The same place soon became a relief center for the students' families who had been affected by the tsunami. Prasit realized he was not alone in his commitment; support poured in from across Thailand. And when the king of Thailand stepped in with help, Prasit said, "I knew a new day was dawning for my school. With His Majesty's help, Bangsak School, now Rajaprajanugroh 35th School, will become a warm shelter, a **sanctuary** for those who are waiting for a brighter day.

Prasit's Additional Survival Skills for Teens

- Don't let bad feelings paralyze you. If you do, you give more power to the bad things in life. Instead, move on.

- Share what you have with others.

---

merited: deserved; earned.

sanctuary: a safe place; a place of protection.

"I vow," said Prasit, "to spend the rest of my life helping my students cross the bridge that will carry them over the destructive waters, so that they can walk with grace toward a life of success and meaning. . . . Loving, caring, sharing, giving: these are the words that give our lives meaning here at Rajaprajanugroh 35th."

Chapter Eight

KEEP YOUR SENSE OF HUMOR

Before Hurricane Katrina, Traemel Day had plans for her life. She was going to get out of the Projects; she was going to save enough money to start her own catering business; she was going to make a better life for herself and her children. Traemel held down a full-time job, took care of her kids, and went to school at New Orleans' Culinary Institute. Book by book, she built up her collection of recipes, knowing that her skill with flour and sugar, rolling pins and ovens, would one day be the foundation for her new life. By August 2005, she was only one course away from her culinary certification.

And then the hurricane hit New Orleans. The Culinary Institute was forced to close. The floodwaters ruined Traemel's collection of recipe books. Traemel and her family fled

Traemel Day
admires her
new home,
provided to her
by Habitat for
Humanity.

to Baton Rouge, leaving behind both their home and Traemel's plans for the future.

But Traemel can still find reasons to laugh—and she does. With the help of the Baton Rouge Habitat for Humanity, Traemel and her children would have a new home, the first of the "homes in a box" that were built across the country. She got a new job as a security guard, and Traemel learned to hope again.

"Katrina is like a love story," she said. "Sometimes it breaks your heart. But sometimes it makes you cry with joy, because you know out of the hardship a brighter future is being born—and there's going to be a happy ending after all. Things are gone in a wink of the eye. You can get angry. Or you can retrain your own mind. Reprogram your thoughts, like a soldier coming back from war. Teach yourself to see the opportunities. Make your eyes see hopeful things. Let it go and smile."

Chapter Nine

CONNECT TO SOMETHING BIGGER THAN YOURSELF

The year 2004 was a hard one for Boon-sruong Dheva-aksorn. The death of her beloved grandfather combined with a series of health problems had left her emotionally and physically drained. A Christmas holiday with her husband and ten-year-old son at the resort of Phang-Nga in Thailand was exactly what she needed to restore her spirits.

On the morning of December 26, Boon-sruong rested in their hotel room while her husband and son enjoyed a swim. Then she heard shouts and screams, and her husband and son burst into the room. Before she could realize what was happening, torrents of ocean water ripped through the front wall of the room.

At first, the family swirled around and around within the room's walls; then all four walls collapsed and the water's suction tore them apart from each other. Buried beneath a mountain of water, Boonsruong struggled to hold her breath. "This is your last breath," she told herself. "Hold it. Hold it for an eternity. If you let go of this last breath, you will be dead." Her desperate thoughts turned into a prayer. In the midst of the water, she asked for the grace and blessing of Buddha and Dharma.

Finally, after being swept more than three hundred feet from the hotel, she grabbed a tree trunk and pulled her head above the water. She sucked in a breath and clung,

Who Is Buddha?

Siddhartha Gautama was a spiritual teacher from ancient India (somewhere between 563 and 483 BCE), who founded the religion of Buddhism and became known as the Buddha. Some Buddhists believe he was a human being who was extremely wise and was able to achieve a degree of enlightenment that few if any other humans have reached. Other Buddhists, however, believe he is an eternal being, the ultimate expression of all that is real and true.

What Is Dharma?

Dharma is a Buddhist concept that describes the underlying order in nature and life. It is the harmony that upholds the world. Peace and happiness in this world are achieved by following the practices of dharma.

A beachfront resort home once stood here on the coast of Thailand. The 2004 tsunami washed away everything but the foundation and the toilet base.

bleeding, exhausted, waiting for the water to recede.

"Buddha teaches that one is one's own refuge," Boonsruong said. "In the midst of destruction, surrounded by debris, [you can]

Why Won't a Buddhist Kill a Cockroach?

Buddhists believe in nonviolence and compassion—and they extend this to even the lowest life forms, including insects, since all life is holy, full of meaning and value. Although human beings sometimes cannot help but kill insects unintentionally, no violence should be committed intentionally.

discard:
to get rid of; throw away.

detached:
separated; disconnected.

gyrating:
spinning; whirling; turning in a circle.

find yourself, even as you **discard** all else." This is what she experienced as she struggled for life in the midst of the tsunami's wave. As her senses returned to her, she looked down and realized her clothes had been swept away by the water, leaving her naked. Strange, **detached** thoughts flickered through her mind: "Naked I was born into this world. When I die, I will be truly naked, for I will have discarded even my own body. Perhaps I am already dead, buried beneath the massive wave. But now I am reborn, naked, just as I was born the first time." For a moment, joy swept through her, followed quickly by fear and sorrow for her family.

An hour later, to her great joy, she and her husband and son were reunited. "We were like cockroaches caught in a toilet bowl," her son said. "Whirling in circles in the water."

As a good Buddhist, Boonsruong never killed the cockroaches she found in their home; instead, she put them in the toilet. "You will not die," she would tell them. "For the time being, **gyrating** in the toilet bowl may be

a bit of a torture—but soon you will be safe in another place." Boonsruong smiled through her tears. She and her family were in a very different place than the one where they had been when they'd woken up that morning on vacation—but at least they were safe.

Boonsruong with her husband and son.

Boonsruong's Additional Survival Skills for Teens

- Find yourself even in the midst of life's chaos—and let go of everything that's not really important.

- Believe that something better will follow your difficult times. No pain lasts forever.

Chapter Ten

BELIEVE IN YOURSELF

Kathy Brown is the sort of person who looks like nothing bad has ever happened to her. She's a smiley woman who loves to eat the pies and cookies she bakes for her family. Her children and husband, her horses and dogs, and the small wallpapering business she runs all make Kathy a happy woman. "My life is good," she said. "Hard to believe now what I lived with as a kid."

Kathy's father was a strict man who ruled his family with an iron hand. "It seemed like I couldn't do anything right when I was a kid," Kathy said. "He was always scolding me about something. Leaving my bike in the driveway. Making a mess in the kitchen. Letting the dog track mud into the house. It was never anything I meant to do wrong. Getting yelled at always took me by surprise. I'd be going along happy as you please—and the next thing I knew, I was in trouble."

Harsh scoldings weren't pleasant, but Kathy and her brother Kevin took them for granted when they were young. Her mother was a good-natured woman, and nothing much seemed to bother her. Kathy and Kevin learned to stay out of their father's way as much as possible. The two siblings were each other's best friends.

Then when Kathy was eleven and her brother was twelve, Kathy and her father had the biggest fight they'd ever had up until that point. "I don't even remember now what it was about," Kathy said. "All I know is I went running out, swearing I was never coming back. I went to a friend's house, and pretty soon I forgot all about it. We were having a good time, playing with Barbie dolls, when the phone rang."

Turned out Kathy's dad had sent Kevin after his sister. Kevin took his bike and went looking for her. He probably would have found her, too—after all, the brother and sister were close to each other and usually knew what the other was thinking—but he forgot to look as he was crossing the busy highway that ran through town. A truck hit him. The ambulance workers said he had been killed instantly.

After that, life changed in the Brown household. Kathy's mother hardly ever spoke. Kathy blamed herself for her brother's death.

And her father blamed her too. Or at least he said he did. "Now that I'm grown up," Kathy told me, "I wonder if he didn't blame himself really. But that was just too painful for him to face. So he took it out on me."

Where before her father had been prone to yelling when he got angry, now his anger was violent. He punched a hole in the living room wall. He kicked the dog. He threw a plate across the kitchen. And then one day, he shoved Kathy so hard she fell down the stairs and broke her collarbone.

That was the first time it happened. Kathy's mother took her to the doctor and made up a lie about how she'd fallen out of a tree. Her mom never seemed to meet Kathy's eyes anymore, though, and Kathy decided her mother blamed her for Kevin's death too. "Maybe, I thought, Mom's glad Dad hurt me. And Dad never even said he was sorry."

After that, her father didn't get angry at Kathy for several months. He seemed to at least be trying to control his temper. But life was still dismal and gloomy in the Brown home, as though Kevin's death had sucked out all the things that had once made them a family. Everything seemed to go wrong. Kathy's father lost his job and had to go on unemployment. The furnace in their house broke, and they didn't have the money to fix it. Then the car broke.

Kathy came up behind her father while he was tinkering with the engine; her mother had asked her to call him in for supper. Maybe she startled him; she never knew for sure. All she knew was that he turned around and hit her with the back of his hand, so hard she remembers that she literally saw stars. Her ears rang for the rest of the evening.

For the next six years, Kathy learned to tiptoe around her father. She tried to fade into the walls; she didn't want to do anything to make him notice her, because if he noticed her, he was apt to hit her. "At first," Kathy said, "I genuinely believed I deserved it. I was so unhappy missing Kevin, and everything seemed so awful. It was like I didn't have a family at all anymore, just these strangers who didn't love me anymore."

As she grew into her teen years, though, Kathy started to get angry too. "I began to hate them, both my mom and my dad. I hated my father for hurting me all the time, I hated my mother for never protecting me. I would lie in bed at night and plot ways of getting even." Kathy stopped working in school, and her grades dropped—but her

Kathy's Additional Survival Skills for Teens

- Don't think things are your fault. No matter what you've done, you don't deserve to be hurt. You deserve to be loved.

- Get help when you need it—and don't give up. Somewhere there's someone who can help you solve your problems.

parents didn't seem to care. She stayed out late with her friends—but her parents never said a word. She began abusing alcohol and experimenting with drugs—but her parents didn't seemed to notice when she came home drunk or high. "I knew then that they really didn't love me," she said. "It was the loneliest feeling, to be fifteen years old and be pretty sure your parents don't care about you."

Luckily, a counselor at Kathy's school took an interest in her. Kathy talked to the counselor—and she also listened to what the counselor had to say. "It wasn't like I woke up one morning and it all clicked into place. It was just this gradual thing, that I slowly started figuring out that if my parents didn't care about me, then I had to care for myself. That I was only hurting myself with all the things I was doing. That it was time to take care of *me*."

When Kathy was seventeen, she moved out of her parents' house, dropped out of school, got a job at the mall, and got an apartment of her own. "I was ready to live my own life," she said. "I made a lot of mistakes—like not finishing school—but I don't really regret any of it. I was doing the best I could." Eventually, she earned her GED and went on to get an associate's degree at the local community college. Today she is married with a family of her own. She believed in herself enough to survive her childhood—and she believes in herself still.

Chapter Eleven

SURRENDER

On a quiet October morning in Pennsylvania's Lancaster County, Emma Mae Zook was teaching her class. The Amish students at the West Nickel Mines one-room schoolhouse ranged in age from young children to teenagers. They all looked up when a man came in the building, mumbling something they couldn't understand. Many of the children may have recognized him as the man who drove the milk truck that stopped each day at their farms. The man went outside, then came back. This time he carried a 9mm handgun in his hand.

The man—whom the world would later learn was Charles Carl Roberts—told the boys in the classroom to help him unload his pickup truck. Emma Mae took the opportunity to escape and run for help. When Roberts saw

Who Are the Amish?

The Amish practice a lifestyle that is uniquely their own, one that sets them apart from the rest of the modern world. The rules of their church cover most aspects of day-to-day living: no power-line electricity, limiting the use of telephones, prohibition of ownership and operation of an automobile, and "plain" dress. The Amish seek to limit contact with the outside world; instead, they emphasize church and family relationships. Amish children attend Amish schools, one-room schoolhouses for children in grades one through eight. About 227,000 Amish currently live in the United States, mostly in Pennsylvania, Indiana, Ohio, and New York State. There are also Amish communities in Ontario, Canada.

her leave, he ordered one of the boys to stop her and threatened to shoot everyone if their teacher got away. Emma Mae had already reached a nearby farm, however, where she asked Amos Smoker to call 911.

Meanwhile, Roberts and the boys carried lumber, a shotgun, a stun gun, wires, chains, nails, tools, and a length of wooden board with multiple sets of metal eyehooks into the classroom. Then, Roberts barricaded the front door, and ordered the girls to line up against the chalkboard. He let a pregnant woman, three parents with babies, and all the male students leave the building; one little girl also escaped: nine-year-old Emma Fisher who spoke only Pennsylvania German, and had not understood Robert's orders. That left ten girls inside with Roberts.

A few minutes later the state troopers arrived as Roberts was binding the arms and legs of his hostages with plastic ties. Roberts warned the troopers to leave immediately, threatening to shoot the girls if they didn't. The police officers backed away and used the loudspeakers in their cruisers to tell Roberts to throw out his weapons and exit the schoolhouse. Roberts refused, again ordering the officers to leave.

By 11:00 a.m. (only a half hour or so after Roberts had first entered the schoolhouse), a crowd that included police officers, emergency medical technicians, and residents of the village had gathered outside the schoolhouse.

Although there was no phone in the schoolhouse, Emma Mae Zook knew that the nearby farm would have a phone where she could call for help. The Amish do not have phones inside their homes, but they do use phones when needed. This farmer has provided an outside phone booth for his Amish neighbors to use.

A typical one-room Amish schoolhouse in Lancaster County, Pennsylvania.

Later, when they were finally safe, the survivors described what had been happening inside the building. The girls talked softly to each other. Two sisters, thirteen-year-old Marian and eleven-year-old Barbie Fisher, asked that they be shot first and that the others be spared. When Roberts opened fire,

Barbie was wounded, while her older sister was killed.

As soon as the troopers heard the gunfire, they ran toward the schoolhouse. As they reached the windows, the shooting abruptly stopped. Roberts had committed suicide.

The troopers broke down the door and carried out the girls. Ambulances and emergency medical technicians rushed to the scene, but three of the girls were already dead.

Two more died early the next morning, leaving five more in critical condition. The youngest victim was six years old, the oldest only thirteen. They had been shot at close range. Lancaster County's deputy coroner told the *Washington Post* that she had counted at least two-dozen bullet wounds in one child alone before she had to stop and ask a colleague to continue for her. Inside the school, she said, "there was not one desk, not one chair, in the whole schoolroom that was not splattered with either blood or glass. There were bullet holes everywhere, everywhere."

coroner: an official who investigates any death suspected of not being due to natural causes.

FORGIVENESS

After the murders, bloggers across the Internet described Roberts as "sick," "evil," "disgusting"—but the people he had hurt the most, the Amish community, reached out with immediate compassion and forgiveness to Roberts' wife and family. On the day of the shooting, a grandfather of one of the murdered Amish girls reminded younger members of the community, "We must not think evil of this man." Another Amish father said, "He had a mother and a wife and a soul and now he's standing before a just God." One of the fathers of the dead girls said, "The pain of the killer's parents is ten times my pain. You would just feel terrible if you were the parent of a killer."

Jack Meyer, a member of another religious community living near the Amish in Lancaster County, explained: "I don't think there's anybody here that wants to do anything but forgive and not only reach out to those who have suffered a loss in that way but to reach out to the family of the man who committed these acts."

The Roberts family was amazed and grateful when Amish community members visited and comforted them. The Amish normally do not mix with others from outside their community, but in this time of terrible tragedy, they reached out past their boundaries. The father of a slain daughter explained, "our forgiveness was not our words, it was what we did." For nearly an hour, one Amish man held Roberts' sobbing father in his arms, comforting him. They hugged Roberts' widow and other members of his family; they brought food and flowers to the Robertses' home. Of the seventy-five people at the killer's burial, over half were Amish, including parents who had buried their own children a day or so before. The Amish community also set up a charitable fund for Roberts' family.

Marie Roberts, the shooter's wife, wrote an open letter to her Amish neighbors, thanking them for their forgiveness:

The New Hope Schoolhouse was built to replace the old one that was a scene of such terrible violence.

> Your love for our family has helped to provide the healing we so desperately need. Gifts you've given have touched our hearts in a way no words can describe. Your compassion has reached beyond our family, beyond our community, and is changing our world, and for this we sincerely thank you.

Some news commentators criticized the Amish community's attitude of such immediate and total forgiveness. Across North

America, many people felt the community's forgiveness made no sense; it even seemed inappropriate. Terrible evil had been done; how could the Amish simply surrender to it. Why were they not reacting with normal, healthy anger?

For the Amish, forgiveness is the first step toward a future that is more hopeful. It is a way of surrendering to whatever life brings, so that you then have the strength to move on. Forgiveness means giving up your right to be angry, to complain, to find a way out, to seek revenge. It means surrendering to the real world—no matter how terrible and awful that world may—so that the world can be transformed into a better place.

In *Amish Grace: How Forgiveness Transcended Tragedy*, Donald Kraybill, with coauthors Steven Nolt and David Weaver-Zercher, wrote:

> For the Amish, . . . the preferred way to live on with meaning and hope is to offer forgiveness—and offer it quickly. That offer, including the willingness to forgo vengeance, does not undo the tragedy or pardon the wrong. It does, however, constitute a first step toward a future that is more hopeful, and potentially less violent, than it would otherwise be.

The Amish's Additional Survival Skill for Teens

- Be willing to forgive those who hurt you.

"If you devote your life to seeking revenge, first dig two graves—yours and your enemy's."

—Confucius

Archbishop Tutu, who survived years of racial violence in South Africa, is another firm believer in the power of surrender to transform both individuals and the world. He writes that surrender allows you to

"Without forgiveness, there's no future."

—Archbishop Tutu

come out on the other side a better person. A better person than the one being consumed by anger and hatred. Remaining in that state locks you in a state of victimhood, making you almost dependent on the perpetrator. If you can find it in yourself to forgive then you are no longer chained to the perpetrator. You can move on, and you can even help the perpetrator to become a better person too.

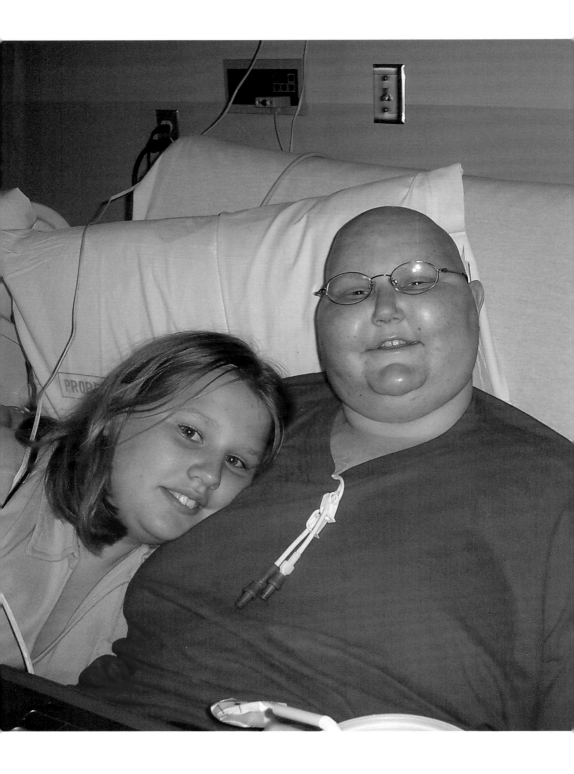

Chapter Twelve

DO WHATEVER IS NECESSARY

L ike Brittany, Bethany is a cancer survivor. Here is Bethany's story:

Cancer changes a person more than you'll ever know. Let me tell you a short story of a very long journey that I have been on while undergoing treatment for Acute Lymphoblastic Leukemia.

Two years ago I started to feel different. My step was slower and every day became harder to handle. I went to my doctor several times. She thought I had the flu. I am overweight, so I thought I was just getting heavier and that I should really go on a diet and exercise more. Then I went back to the doctor, this time with crushing bone pain that ibuprofen and Tylenol wouldn't touch. I became weaker

leukemia:
a cancer of the blood or blood-forming organs (bone marrow) marked by an increase in the number of white blood cells called leukocytes.

morphine pump:
a device used to intravenously deliver morphine, a pain medication.

and weaker as they tried to figure out what was wrong. By the end of the day, the doctors in the small local hospital where I had been taken told me they suspected I had **leukemia**. That night I was hooked up to a **morphine pump** to help make me more comfortable. I could tell that my family was very scared. I don't think I would have been so frightened if I hadn't seen my mom crying. She is my security blanket and usually puts on a brave face no matter what we're up against. The doctor told me that the next day I would be transported to Strong Hospital in Rochester, New York. I should have gone that day but the weather was too stormy.

The next day, after I was settled into my new room at Strong, my primary

Bethany receiving oxygen during one of her treatment's many complications.

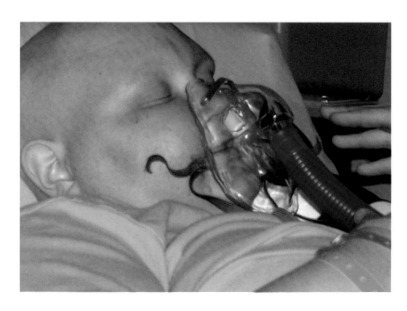

oncologist, Dr. David Korones, came in to tell me that I had cancer. I asked if it was curable, and he said yes it was. I told him that I would eat kitty litter if it would help me to get better, and that it was time to get started! Little did I know what I was about to go through and how much my life as I knew it was about to change.

When I first lost my hair, I'll admit I was pretty devastated, but that lasted about a day. After that it became fun having no hair. Everyone thought that I was so cute. After my mom cut it she said, "Tweety! My baby!" (She always thought I had looked like Tweety Bird when I was little because of my big eyes, long eyelashes, and the one or two strands of hair on my head—and now I looked like that again.) Being bald was also very convenient: I didn't have to wash my hair anymore. One of the best parts was scaring people as we drove by them in the car! No, I didn't care about the hair that much. I was more concerned about my health.

I have experienced a number of serious complications and side effects to medications over the past two years, including an **anaphylactic** allergic reaction to a chemotherapy drug, **chemical hepatitis**, the formation of three large blood clots in my heart, along with **pulmonary emboli**, kidney stones, **gastritis**,

anaphylactic: related to anaphylaxis, an extreme allergic reaction to a foreign substance.

chemical hepatitis: inflammation of the liver caused by drugs or other chemicals.

pulmonary: relating to the lungs.

emboli: masses, such as air bubbles, blood clots, or other foreign matter, in the bloodstream that cause obstructions in blood vessels.

gastritis: an inflammation or irritation of the stomach lining.

Bethany today.

compression fractures: the breaking and collapse of bone tissue in the vertebrae due to injury, disease, or bone degradation caused by certain drugs.

seven **compression fractures** in my spine which confined me to a wheelchair for a couple of months, and necrosis of the hip, which will require a total hip replacement. I gained forty pounds through steroid treatment and a drug called asparaginase—but don't worry: then I lost fifty pounds after throwing up almost nonstop for three straight months.

I've learned so much these past two years. Cancer has helped me grow up into the person I've always wanted to be, decide what I believe in, and determine what I want out of life. This illness has made me think about the way the world works and how interconnected everything is. I learned how much the world takes for granted too. Simple things like taking a shower, brushing my teeth, and walking up the stairs are amazing luxuries and require a lot more strength than you think. Every day I wake up, I am thankful that I'm alive!

Bethany's Additional Survival Skills for Teens

- Don't take yourself too seriously.

- Don't take simple pleasures for granted.

- Remember, your goal is worth everything you're putting up with now.

Chapter Thirteen

NEVER
GIVE UP

Malaysia's eastern island, Borneo, is the third largest island in the world. Borneo is home to thick rain forests and towering mountains. One particularly impressive peak that northern Borneo boasts is called Mount Kinabalu, and within its slopes lies Low's Gully. A gully is simply the name given to any deep ravine or cut in the earth, usually made by some movement of water—a river or waterfall, for instance. In the case of Low's Gully, three different waterfalls flow down into the gully's bottom and accumulate in a few small ponds. The walls of the gully are both rocky and steep, many of them almost entirely vertical, making the gully difficult and dangerous to get into.

A British army training expedition under the command of Lieutenant-Colonel Robert Neill accepted Low's Gully's challenge. The ten-member team had climbed Kinabalu and spent a few days learning mountain survival skills before descending into the gully.

In 1851, Sir Hugh Low, a British Colonial Secretary, had set out to explore Mount Kinabalu with a traveling party of about forty men. Low discovered that on the slope was what he called "a circular amphitheatre" into which he could not find an end. In other words, he and his men had stumbled upon a massive gully. Many of the men with Low were native to the island, and they told him of legends surrounding the mountain and this very gully. The legends spoke of a wronged dragon that lived deep in this "cave" (gully) in order to guard a huge jewel. The native men said that explorers had tried to steal the dragon's jewel and as a result it had cursed this mountain and any who attempted to conquer it.

But the ten men descending the gully on February 22, 1994, cared little about the legend. They were looking for exercise and adventure, not precious stones. When the team began the descent, they broke into two smaller teams of five, one led by Neill and the other by another officer, Private Mayfield, who was the most experienced climber in the group. Unfortunately, because of bad communication and lesser climbing experience, Neill and his team soon fell well behind Mayfield's crew.

Neill was worried from the beginning about the rate of progress they were making down the slope, and by day six of the descent his fears were confirmed: they had completely lost contact with Mayfield's team. They emerged from a wooded portion of the slope onto a granite surface, and for the first time were able to look straight to the bottom of the gully. Mayfield's crew was nowhere to be seen. Where had they gone? The slope was steep enough that Neill was forced to question whether the other team had attempted it at all. After **assessing** the situation, Neill decided they had most likely continued downward. He then decided his team's only choice was to follow after them.

This proved a more difficult task than expected. Without Mayfield, Neill's team **abseiled** down the slope only a few dozen feet at a time, and to complicate things even further, the weather turned foul, and rain began to fall. The climbers now risked further injury on a slick surface. By day 10 the slope gave way to yet another vertical drop. In Neill's own words: "We were looking at air." Rations were running low, and things were not looking good.

At this point the five-man team consisted of two British officers, Neill and his second-in-command Ron Foster, and three Hong Kong soldiers. Neill decided it was best to halt all operations; the rest of the crew were relieved to hear this decision. After some thought, it was decided they should attempt to retreat back up the gully. But this proved impossible. Rain was falling hard and the climbers

assessing:
sizing up; determining the significance or importance of.

abseiled:
rappelled.

began looking desperately for shelter. One of the men, Kevin Cheung, found a cave.

At first, the men were delighted to find shelter from the rain. Little did they know, they would come to know this cave much more intimately than they ever imagined. It would form a crude base camp for the next three weeks. In his book *Survival*, Anthony Masters recounts the journal entries of both Foster and Neill. Foster gives the following reasons for remaining in the cave:

- Water too dangerous to carry on.
- Hong Kong soldiers need rest.
- Several minor injuries.
- Any escape must be planned properly in view of our failed attempt yesterday.
- Conserve energy and rations.
- We are by water.
- We have shelter.
- Liew [one of the Hong Kong soldiers] said helicopters available.
- We can be seen from the air.
- This is the most suitable spot in this part of the gully for a helicopter to get in.

Their team was already two days late for their return to headquarters, and they hoped this would alert the Malaysians to begin a search for them. On March 7, the weather finally cleared, and Neill and Foster began gathering slate-gray rocks to form a giant

Caves can
sometimes
make good
shelters.

"SOS" on the mossy green surface of the gully. Foster also made the number "5" out of stones to indicate there were five people in need of help. Along with the stones, they laid out pieces of aluminum to reflect light and a red equipment bag to attract any rescuers' eyes.

In the meantime, Neill pondered the fate of the other five-man team. He wondered where they had gone and how the two teams had been separated. He felt intense guilt for getting his men into this life-threatening situation. One of his biggest concerns, of course, was rations: they had to be given out each day in smaller and smaller portions. Soon they would be gone completely. And without food, would the men be strong enough to climb out of the gully themselves, if it came down to that? Neill was determined to get them out. He was not going to give up.

On March 11, Neill and Foster departed from the cave in order to look for a way out. The two officers, along with the rest of the men, were in bad physical shape. But they needed to do something. Very quickly, however, Neill and Foster realized how difficult it was to cut through the jungle lining the gully's walls. It was harder still to climb the steep embankments, and eventually they came to the end of their efforts when they faced a totally vertical wall of mud and loose stone. Both admitted defeat this time around—but if they had lost a battle, they refused to accept that they'd lost the war.

Any kind of terrain or climate has its own survival challenges.

The next morning, however, brought hope when they were awoken by the sound of a helicopter. They immediately scrambled to signal it, Foster rapidly firing the flash of his camera and both laying out any reflective equipment they had on the ground. They returned to the cave with **optimism**, but after several days of waiting, they realized the helicopter had not seen them. Help was not on its way.

Back at the cave, conditions were worsening. The men were slowly starving. The only nutrition they had left were salt and sugar supplements, and a few **glucose** tablets. Their clothes and bedding were wet and rotting, providing less shelter and exposing them to more disease by the day.

On Saturday, March 19, Foster made a decision to go out on his own for one last attempt to escape. Foster was bigger and heavier built than the rest of the men, and he was determined. He set out on March 20, and his desperation pushed him up an incredible 70-degree slope. Struggling through thick vegetation and using dangerous footholds, Foster used up the last of his strength while still some hundred feet below the gully's ridge. That night he fell into an exhausted sleep.

The next morning, he awoke to the sound of a helicopter. This time the helicopter remained for a longer period of time, but again it took off and disappeared. Feeling discouraged, Foster returned to the cave.

optimism: a belief that good things will come.

glucose: a sugar; the body's main energy source.

The sounds and sight of a helicopter brought initial hope to Neill and Foster, but they despaired when the helicopter left again, without any sign that their signals had been seen.

The next few nights were the darkest yet. The smell of rotting boots and clothes filled the air. Neill noticed his urine had now turned from dark yellow to an even darker brown. Clean water was scarce, and both disease and **dehydration** were looming. Neill still refused to give up, but it was harder and harder to feel hopeful.

Then on Friday, March 25, the thirtieth day in the gully, a helicopter arrived and hovered directly above their camp. There was no mistaking it this time: the people in the helicop-

dehydration: an excessive loss of water from the body.

Neill and Foster's Additional Survival Skills for Teens

- Accept that you've made mistakes—and keep going.

- Don't worry if you feel discouraged. Discouragement is natural—but don't let it interfere with your determination to hold on.

"This awful catastrophe is not the end but the beginning."

—St. Augustine

ter had seen them! As if from heaven, a bag of rations with a note tied to it dropped from the helicopter . . . only to land in a pool of water. They were able to salvage the food, though, but the only part of the note was still legible: "HELP IS ON ITS WAY. ENCLOSED ARE RATIONS. HANG ON IN THERE LADS."

The men had been saved. Soon after, the entire party, including the missing team members, was lifted out of the cave and taken to safety. Neill's determination had paid off.

Further Reading

Espeland, Pamela. *Life Lists for Teens: Tips, Steps, Hints, and How-Tos for Growing Up, Getting Along, Learning, and Having Fun*. Minneapolis, Minn.: Freespirit, 2003.

Fox, Annie. *The Teen Survival Guide To Dating & Relating: Real-World Advice on Guys, Girls, Growing Up, and Getting Along*. Minneapolis, Minn.: Freespirit, 2005.

————. *Too Stressed To Think? A Teen Guide To Staying Sane When Life Makes You Crazy*. Minneapolis, Minn.: Freespirit, 2005.

Gonzales, Laurence. *Deep Survival: Who Lives, Who Dies, and Why*. New York: Norton, 2004.

————. *Everyday Survival*. New York: Norton, 2008.

Metcalf, C. W. *Lighten Up: Survival Skills for People Under Pressure*. New York: Basic Books, 2003.

Wiseman, John. *SAS Survival Handbook: How to Survive in the Wild, in Any Climate, on Land or at Sea*. New York: Collins, 2004.

For More Information

Adolescent Development
www.etr.org/recapp/theories/
AdolescentDevelopment/index.htm

Adolescent Growth and Development
www.ext.vt.edu/pubs/family/350-850/
350-850.html

Blackfire
www.blackfire.net

Dealing with Peer Pressure
kidshealth.org/kid/feeling/emotion/peer_
pressure.html

Stress Management Skills for Teens
at-risk-youth-support.suite101.com/article.
cfm/stress_management_skills_for_teens

Publisher's note:
The Web sites listed on this page were active
at the time of publication. The publisher is not
responsible for Web sites that have changed
their addresses or discontinued operation
since the date of publication. The publisher
will review and update the Web-site list upon
each reprint.

Bibliography

Gonzales, Laurence. *Deep Survival: Who Lives, Who Dies, and Why*. New York: Norton, 2004.

Henslin, James. *Essentials of Sociology*, 6th ed. Boston: Allyn and Bacon, 2006.

Kraybill, Donald B., Steven M. Nolt, and David L. Weaver. *Amish Grace: How Forgiveness Transcended Tragedy*. San Francisco: Jossey-Bass, 2007.

Life Books. *Nature's Fury: Wild Weather & Natural Disasters*. New York: Life, 2008.

Ripley, Amanda. *The Unthinkable: Who Survives When Disaster Strikes—and Why*. New York: Crown, 2008.

Tennant, Victoria. "Understanding the Mysteries of the Teenage Brain." 2007. Available online at casat.unr.edu/docs/Understanding_the_Teenage_Brain.doc.

Tutu, Desmond. *No Future Without Forgiveness*. New York: Doubleday, 1999.

Weiss, Elaine. *Surviving Domestic Violence: Voices of Women Who Broke Free*. Scottsdale, Ariz.: Agreka Books, 2000.

Wilson, K.J. *When Violence Begins at Home: A Comprehensive Guide to Understanding and Ending Domestic Abuse*. 2nd ed. Alameda, Calif.: Hunter House Publishers, 2006.

Bibliography

Zullo, Alan and Mara Bovsun. *Survivors: True Stories of Children in the Holocaust*. New York: Scholastic, 2005.

Index

Index

AR (Aktion Reinhard Camps). www. deathcamps.org: p. 54

cc-a 2.0
Deger, Steve: p. 115

cc-a-ndw 2.0
jrwebbe: p. 110

Dheva-aksorn, Boonsruong: p. 87

Dreamstime Images:
Corot2: p. 28
Gadjoboy: p. 94
Gunion, Richard: p. 99
Jensen, Derek: p. 97
Li, Wa: p. 69
Palangsi: p. 88

EarthStation1.com
Kaelin, J. C. Jr.: p. 52, 57, 61

Harding House Publishing, Inc.
Stewart, Benjamin: p. 34, 36, 42, 45, 46, 49, 72, 75, 80, 82, 85

istockphoto.com
Friedman, Rob: p. 32
steidl, james: p. 12

Jupiter Images: p. 8, 11, 16, 118

NASA: p. 78

National Biological Information Infrastructure Public Domain.
Randolph Femmer: p. 117

Therrien, Patricia: p. 64, 104, 106, 108

United States Air Force
Snyder, Jonathan: p. 26

Zwoje-scrolls.com: p. 58

To the best knowledge of the publisher, all images not specifically credited are in the public domain. If any image has been inadvertently uncredited, please notify Harding House Publishing Service, 220 Front Street, Vestal, New York 13850, so that credit can be given in future printings.

About the Author and the Consultant

Author

Rae Simons is the author of many young adult books. She lives in New York State with her teenage children.

Consultant

Andrew M. Kleiman, M.D. is a Clinical Instructor in Psychiatry at New York University School of Medicine. He received a BA in philosophy from the University of Michigan, and graduated from Tulane University School of Medicine. Dr. Kleiman completed his internship, residency, and fellowship in psychiatry at New York University and Bellevue Hospital. He is currently in private practice in Manhattan and teaches at New York University School of Medicine.